BOOK • VIDEO

WARREN HAYNES

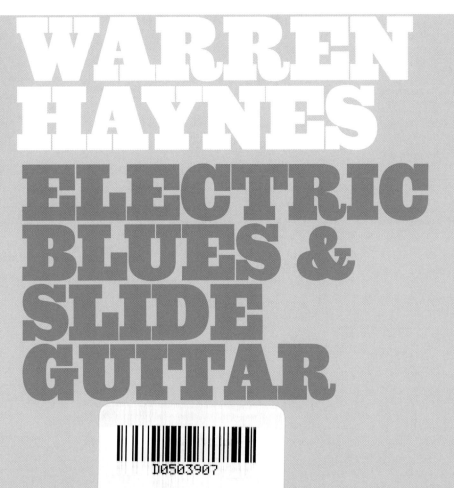

ELECTRIC BLUES & SLIDE GUITAR

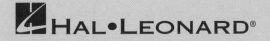

D0503907

To access video visit:
www.halleonard.com/mylibrary

Enter Code
4567-0193-6421-9336

ISBN: 978-1-5400-2039-0

HAL•LEONARD®

Copyright © 1994, 2005, 2018 Music Sales Corporation
International Copyright Secured All Rights Reserved

No part of this publication may be reproduced in any form or by
any means without the prior written permission of the Publisher.

Visit Hal Leonard Online at
www.halleonard.com

Contact us:
Hal Leonard
7777 West Bluemound Road
Milwaukee, WI 53213
Email: info@halleonard.com

In Europe, contact:
Hal Leonard Europe Limited
42 Wigmore Street
Marylebone, London, W1U 2RN
Email: info@halleonardeurope.com

In Australia, contact:
Hal Leonard Australia Pty. Ltd.
4 Lentara Court
Cheltenham, Victoria, 3192 Australia
Email: info@halleonard.com.au

GUITAR NOTATION LEGEND

Guitar music can be notated three different ways: on a *musical staff*, in *tablature*, and in *rhythm slashes*.

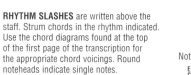

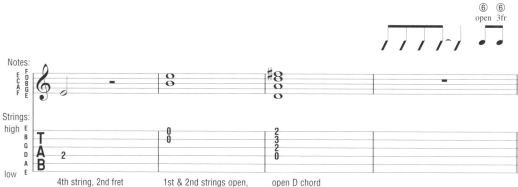

RHYTHM SLASHES are written above the staff. Strum chords in the rhythm indicated. Use the chord diagrams found at the top of the first page of the transcription for the appropriate chord voicings. Round noteheads indicate single notes.

THE MUSICAL STAFF shows pitches and rhythms and is divided by bar lines into measures. Pitches are named after the first seven letters of the alphabet.

TABLATURE graphically represents the guitar fingerboard. Each horizontal line represents a string, and each number represents a fret.

HALF-STEP BEND: Strike the note and bend up 1/2 step.

WHOLE-STEP BEND: Strike the note and bend up one step.

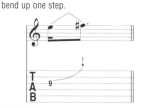

GRACE NOTE BEND: Strike the note and immediately bend up as indicated.

SLIGHT (MICROTONE) BEND: Strike the note and bend up 1/4 step.

BEND AND RELEASE: Strike the note and bend up as indicated, then release back to the original note. Only the first note is struck.

PRE-BEND: Bend the note as indicated, then strike it.

VIBRATO: The string is vibrated by rapidly bending and releasing the note with the fretting hand.

WIDE VIBRATO: The pitch is varied to a greater degree by vibrating with the fretting hand.

HAMMER-ON: Strike the first (lower) note with one finger, then sound the higher note (on the same string) with another finger by fretting it without picking.

PULL-OFF: Place both fingers on the notes to be sounded. Strike the first note and without picking, pull the finger off to sound the second (lower) note.

LEGATO SLIDE: Strike the first note and then slide the same fret-hand finger up or down to the second note. The second note is not struck.

SHIFT SLIDE: Same as legato slide, except the second note is struck.

TRILL: Very rapidly alternate between the notes indicated by continuously hammering on and pulling off.

TAPPING: Hammer ("tap") the fret indicated with the pick-hand index or middle finger and pull off to the note fretted by the fret hand.

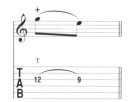

NATURAL HARMONIC: Strike the note while the fret-hand lightly touches the string directly over the fret indicated.

PINCH HARMONIC: The note is fretted normally and a harmonic is produced by adding the edge of the thumb or the tip of the index finger of the pick hand to the normal pick attack.

PICK SCRAPE: The edge of the pick is rubbed down (or up) the string, producing a scratchy sound.

MUFFLED STRINGS: A percussive sound is produced by laying the fret hand across the string(s) without depressing, and striking them with the pick hand.

PALM MUTING: The note is partially muted by the pick hand lightly touching the string(s) just before the bridge.

RAKE: Drag the pick across the strings indicated with a single motion.

TREMOLO PICKING: The note is picked as rapidly and continuously as possible.

VIBRATO BAR DIVE AND RETURN: The pitch of the note or chord is dropped a specified number of steps (in rhythm), then returned to the original pitch.

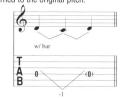

VIBRATO BAR SCOOP: Depress the bar just before striking the note, then quickly release the bar.

VIBRATO BAR DIP: Strike the note and then immediately drop a specified number of steps, then release back to the original pitch.

CONTENTS

Tuning

Biography 4

Selected Discography 5

Electric Guitar Intro

Chapter 1: Attack and Vibrato 6
Examples 1-10

Chapter 2: String Bending 9
Examples 11-18

Chapter 3: Varying the Harmonic Structure 11
Examples 19-25

Chapter 4: Notes Outside the Blues Scale 14
Examples 26-34

Chapter 5: Rhythmic Phrasing 25
Examples 35-40

Slide Guitar Intro

Chapter 6: Fingerpicking and Damping 32
Examples 41-48

Chapter 7: Light Touch 35
Examples 49-52

Chapter 8: Choosing Strings for Tone 36
Examples 53-56

Chapter 9: Emulating Open-Tuned Sounds in Standard Tuning . . . 37
Examples 57-61

Chapter 10: Vibrato and Intonation 41
Examples 62-73

Outro and Credits

BIOGRAPHY

Guitarist, singer, and songwriter Warren Haynes grew up listening to soul music, initially focusing on the vocal music of Memphis and Motown singers like Levi Stubbs, Wilson Pickett, and Otis Redding. It wasn't long before a young Haynes discovered guitar and widened his focus to include the music of blues hero B.B. King and rock legend Eric Clapton.

By age 14, Haynes was offered the stage at a local club for his first performance. He soon formed his first band, Ricochet, which gathered a regional following. His first major break, however, came when appeared on Dickey Betts's 1986 solo album, *Pattern Disruptive*, and in the same year co-wrote the title track on Gregg Allman's *Just Before the Bullets Fly*.

In 1989, as the Allman Brothers Band was planning a comeback, they chose Haynes as their new guitarist, and his fiery blues and rock guitar breathed new life into the band. Haynes was already making a name for himself among some of the most well-respected rock giants of all time.

In the years that followed, the Allman Brothers Band, with Haynes firmly entrenched, released three studio albums, two live sets, and gained four GRAMMY® nominations, including a 1995 win for a live version of "Jessica."

In 1992, while also playing with the Allman Brothers Band, Haynes released his first solo album, *Tales of Ordinary Madness*. Two years later, Haynes and Allman Brothers bassist Allen Woody formed Gov't Mule, with Matt Abts on drums. The trio's basic improvisational blues style was an instant hit with fans. They released their self-titled debut in 1995, followed by Live at Roseland Ballroom in 1996.

The following year, Haynes and Woody decided to focus on the growing success of Gov't Mule and resigned from the Allman Brothers Band. Gov't Mule released their third album, Dose, in 1998, immediately followed by *Live...With a Little Help from Our Friends*, in 1999. The band's fifth release, *Life Before Insanity*, was issued in early 2000.

Soon after that release, Woody passed away. Haynes and Abts then put out a tribute to Woody with *The Deep End: Volumes I and II*, on which the pair was joined by guest bassists including John Entwistle, Flea, and Mike Gordon.

After a short stint as guitarist and singer for Phil Lesh and Friends, Haynes rejoined the Allman Brothers Band in 2001. He was co-writer on nine original tracks on the band's 2003 album *Hittin' the Note*.

SELECTED DISCOGRAPHY

Warren Haynes

Tales of Ordinary Madness (Megaforce, 1992)

The Lone EP (ATO, 2003)

Live at Bonnaroo (ATO, 2004)

Dickey Betts

Pattern Disruptive (Epic, 1986)

Gregg Allman

Just Before the Bullets Fly (Epic, 1988)

Gov't Mule

Gov't Mule (Relativity, 1995)

Live at Roseland Ballroom (Foundation, 1996)

Dose (Capricorn, 1998)

Live...With a Little Help from Our Friends (Capricorn, 1999)

Life Before Insanity (Polygram, 2000)

The Deep End: Volume I (ATO, 2001)

The Deep End: Volume II (ATO, 2002)

Live...With a Little Help from Our Friends, Vol. 2 (Evangeline, 2002)

The Deepest End: Live in Concert (ATO, 2003)

Allman Brothers Band

Seven Turns (Epic, 1990)

Shades of Two Worlds (Epic, 1991)

An Evening With the Allman Brothers Band: First Set (Epic, 1992)

Where It All Begins (Epic, 1994)

An Evening With the Allman Brothers Band: Second Set (Epic, 1995)

Hittin' the Note (Peach/Sanctuary, 2003)

One Way Out (Peach/Sanctuary, 2004)

Déja Voodoo (ATO, 2004)

Chapter 1: Attack and Vibrato

Example 1
(:14)

Example 2
(2:13)

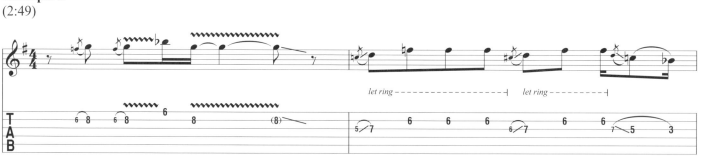

Example 3
(2:49)

Example 4
(3:05)

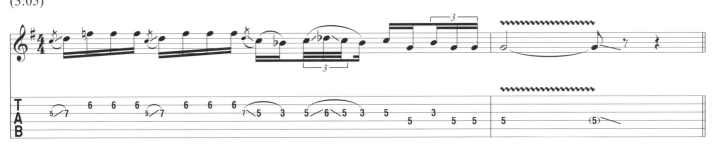

Example 5: Faster Vibrato
(3:42)

Example 6: Slower Vibrato
(3:52)

Example 7
(4:31)

Example 8
(4:51)

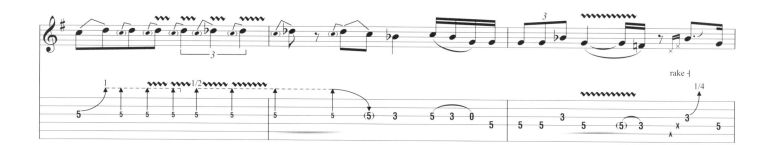

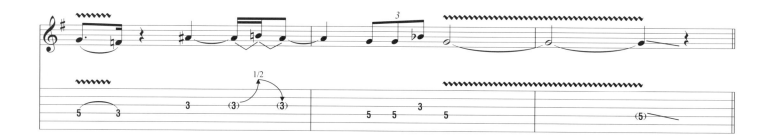

Example 9
(5:40)

Example 10
(6:54)

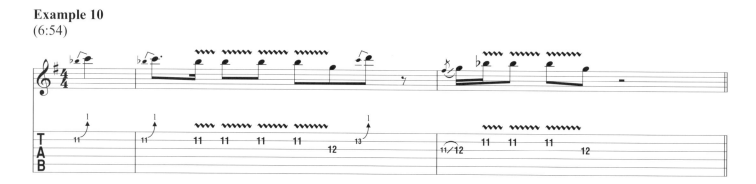

8

Chapter 2: String Bending

Example 11A: Albert King Lick
(1:12)

Example 11B
(1:18)

Example 11C
(1:23)

Example 12
(2:06)

Example 13
(3:08)

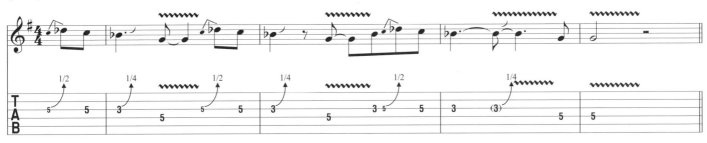

Example 14
(3:44)

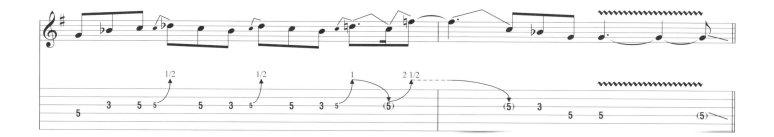

Example 15
(4:37)

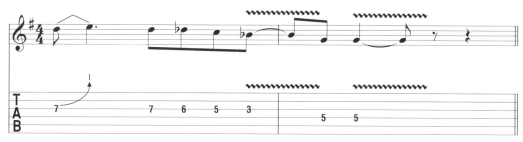

Example 16
(4:45)

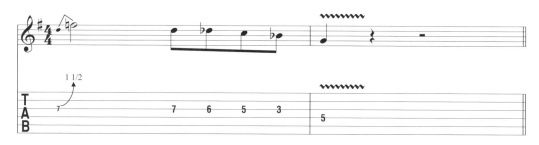

Example 17
(4:54)

Example 18
(5:36)

Chapter 3: Varying the Harmonic Structure

Example 19
(:24)

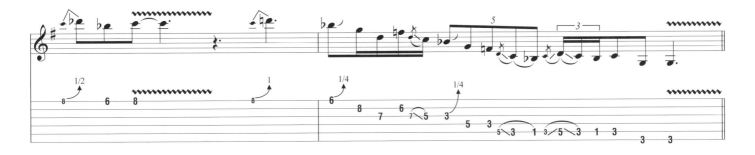

Example 20
(1:07)

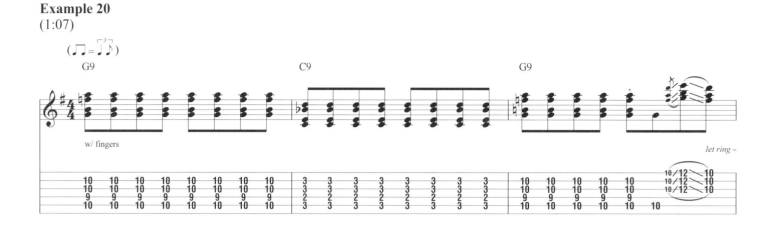

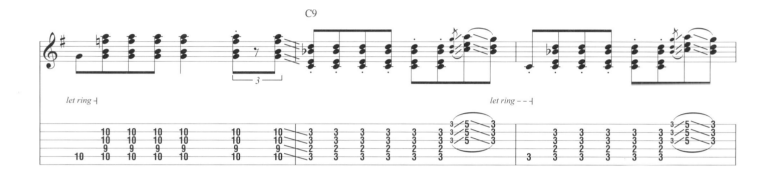

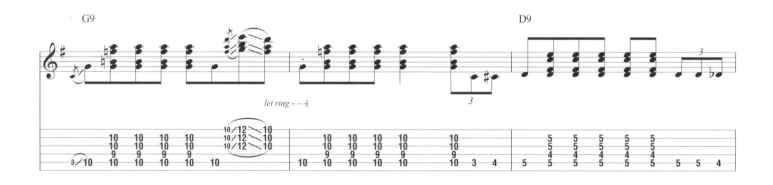

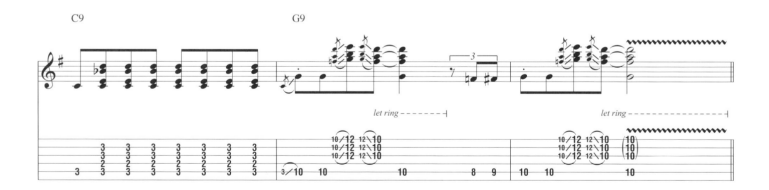

Example 21
(2:08)

Example 22
(2:25)

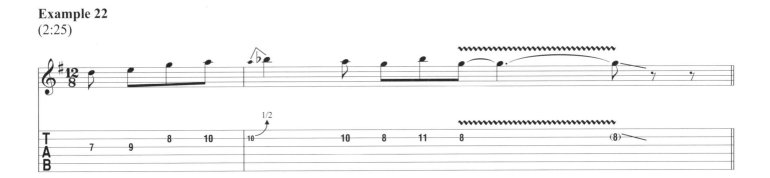

Example 23
(3:17)

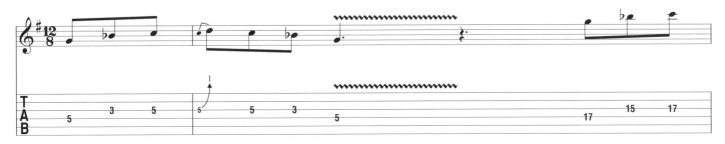

Example 24

(5:05)

Example 25

(6:05)

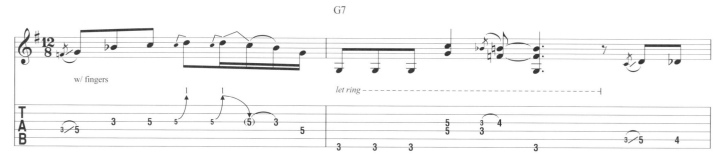

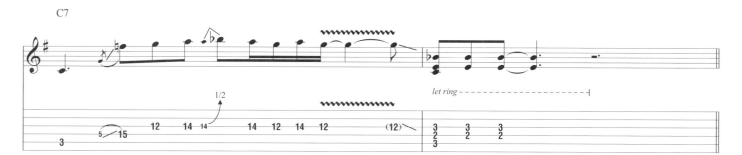

Chapter 4: Notes Outside the Blues Scale

Example 26

(:39)

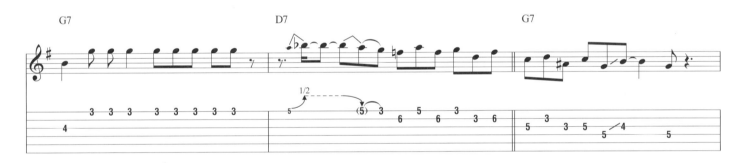

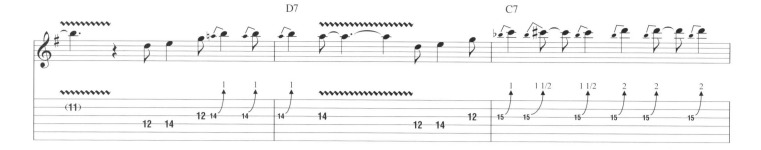

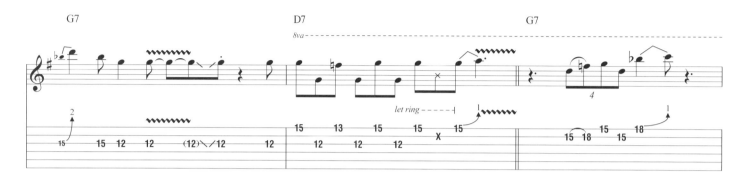

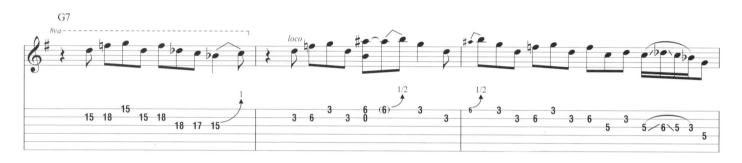

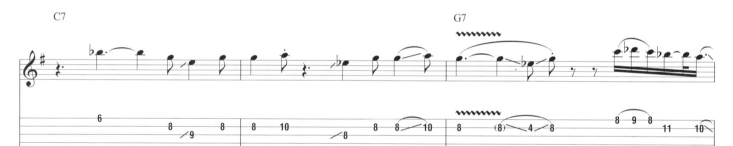

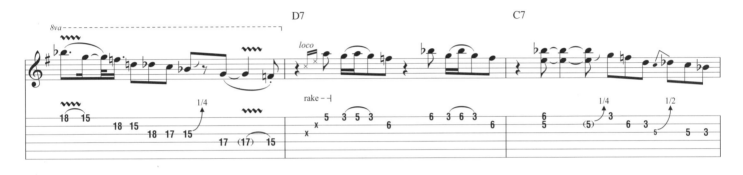

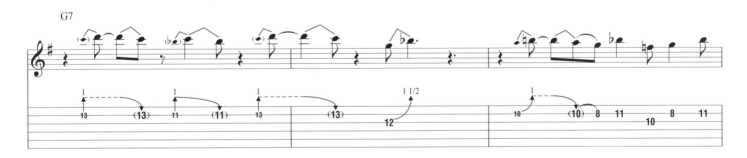

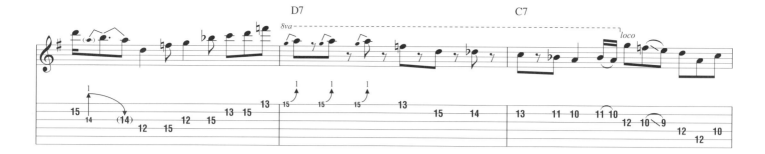

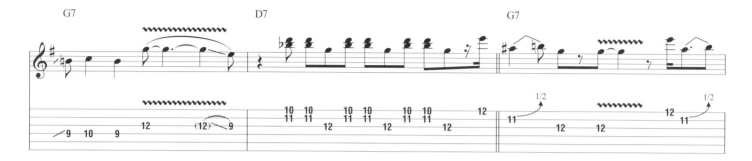

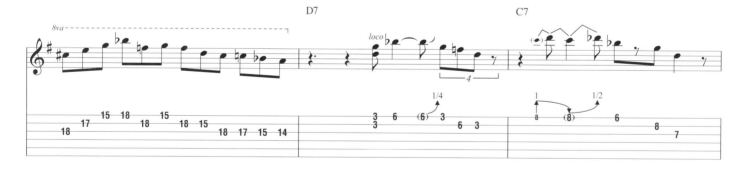

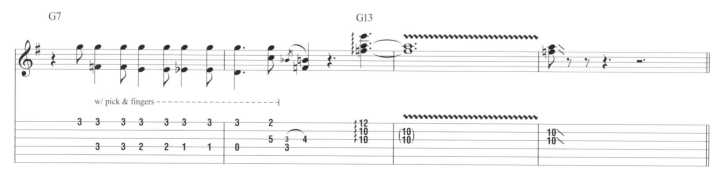

Example 27
(3:36)

Example 28
(3:53)

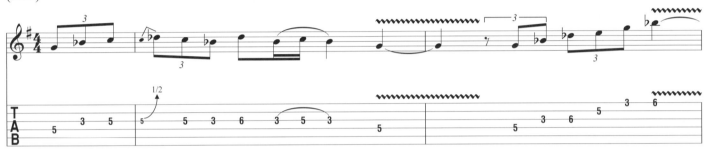

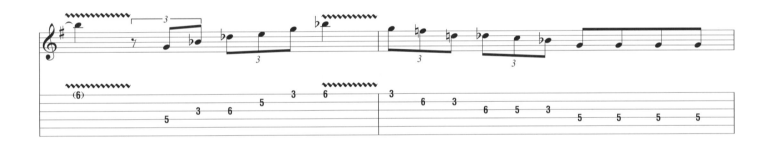

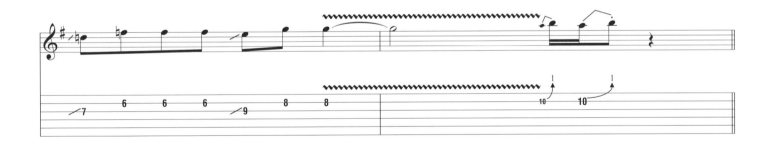

Example 29
(4:32)

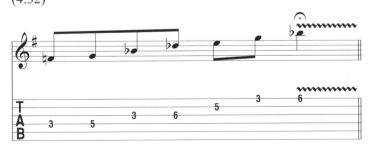

Example 30
(4:52)

Example 31
(6:38)

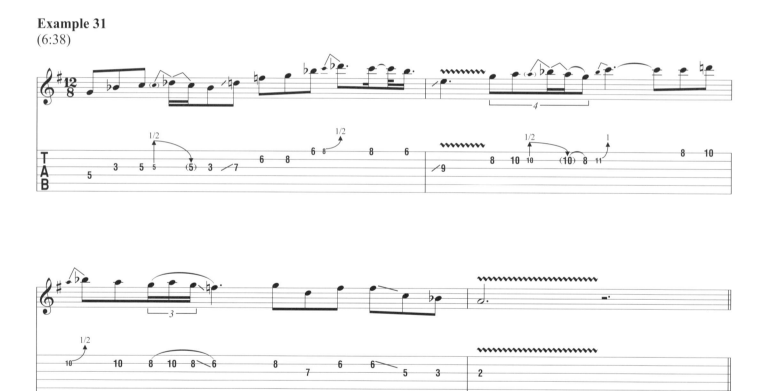

Example 32
(7:32)

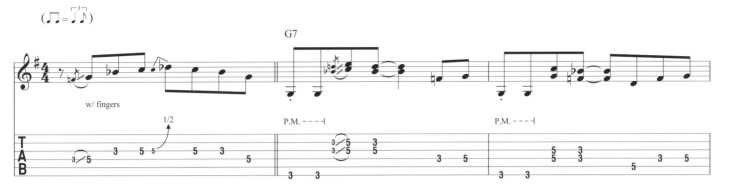

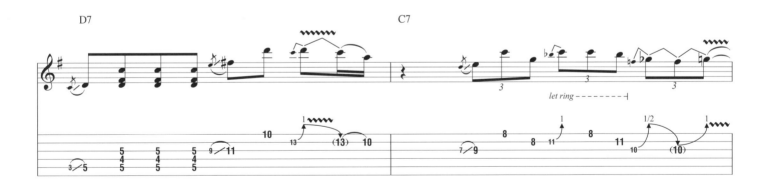

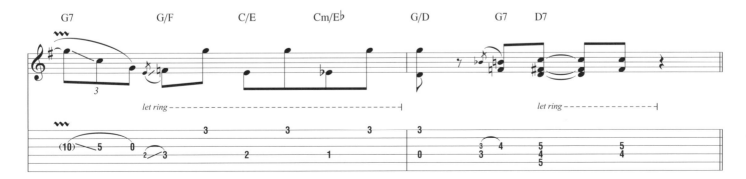

Example 33
(8:21)

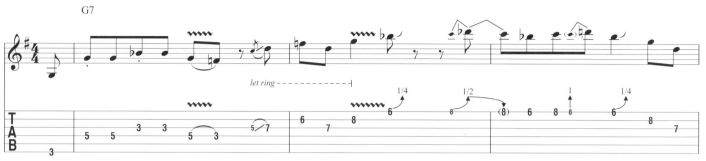

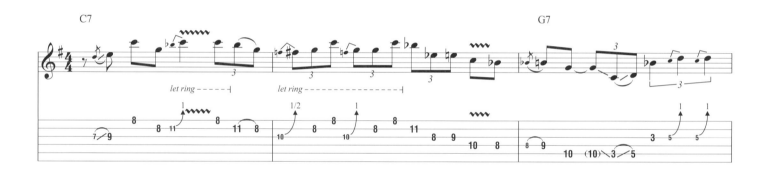

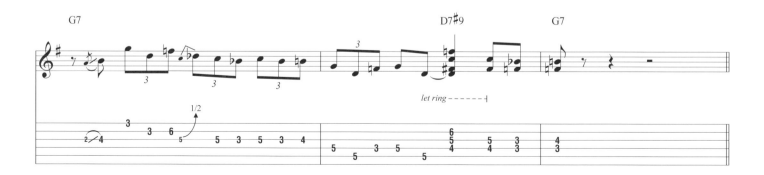

Example 34
(9:20)

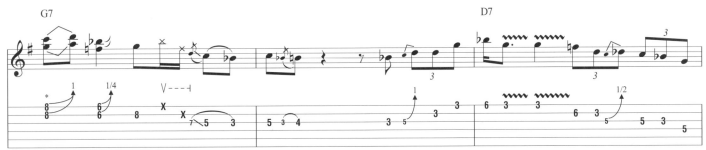

*2nd string caught under bend finger.

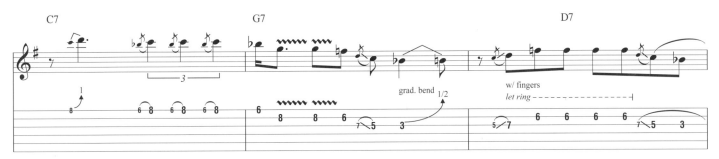

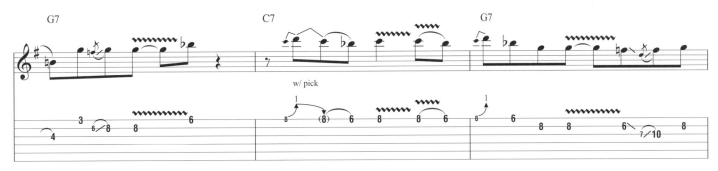

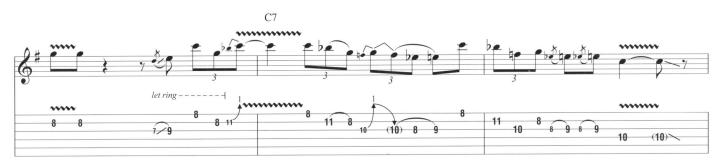

23

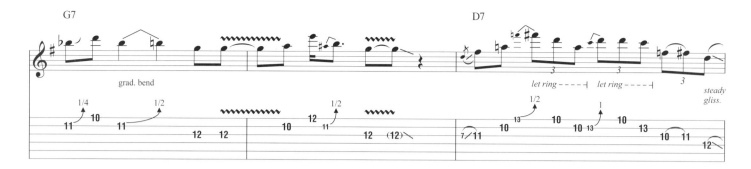

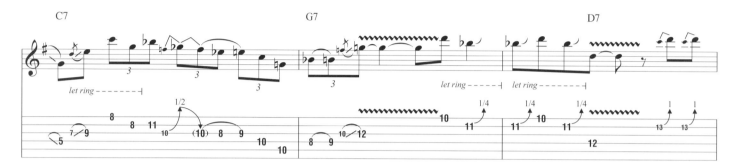

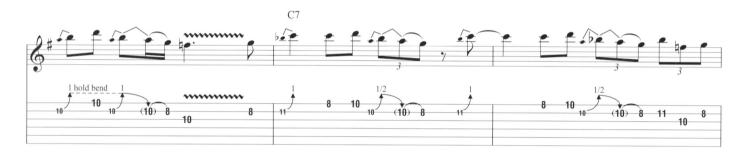

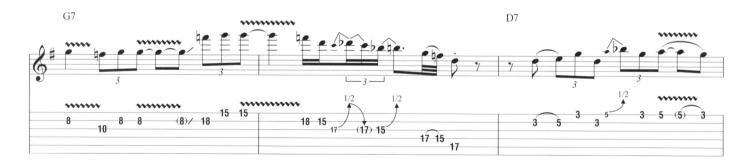

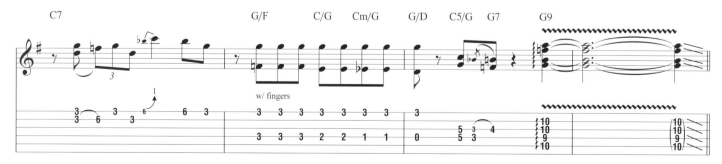

Chapter 5: Rhythmic Phrasing

Example 35
(:23)

Example 36
(:30)

Example 37
(:38)

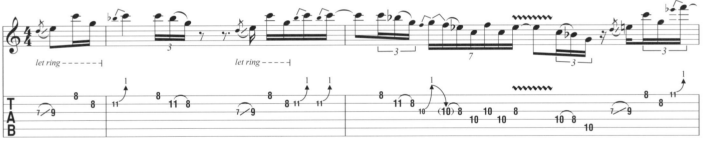

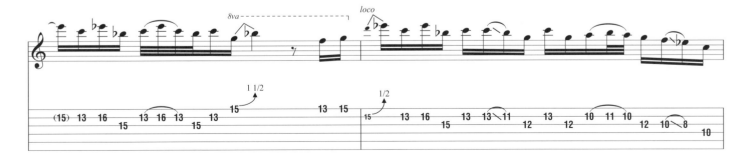

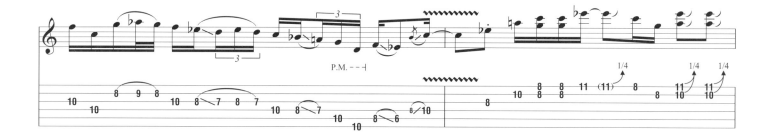

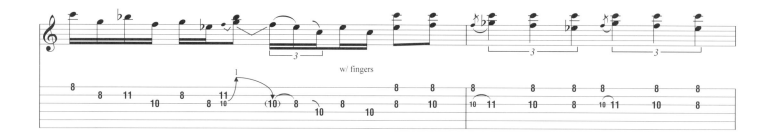

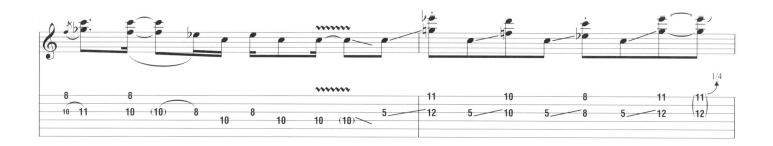

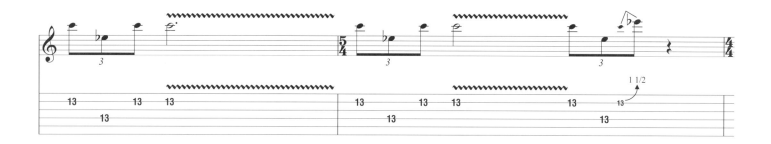

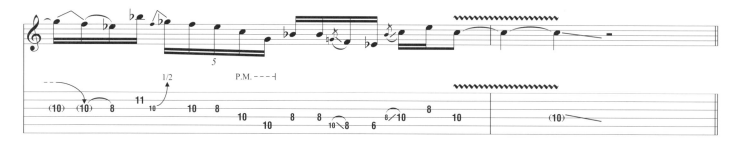

Example 38
(1:28)

*2nd string caught under bend finger.

Example 39
(2:07)

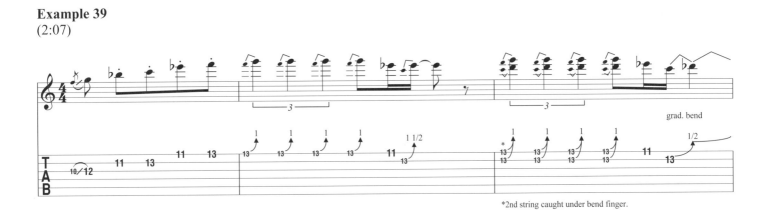

grad. bend

*2nd string caught under bend finger.

Example 40
(2:45)

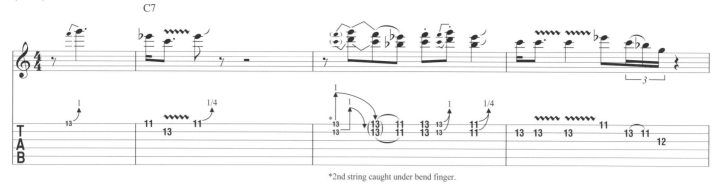

*2nd string caught under bend finger.

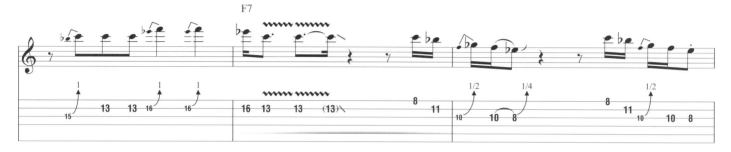

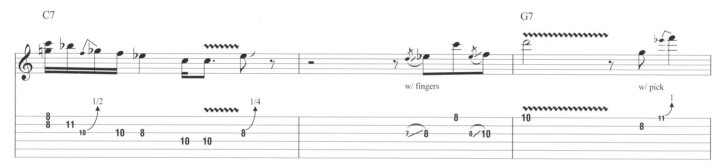

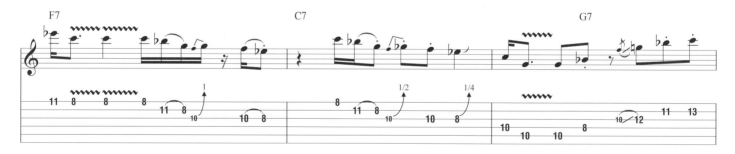

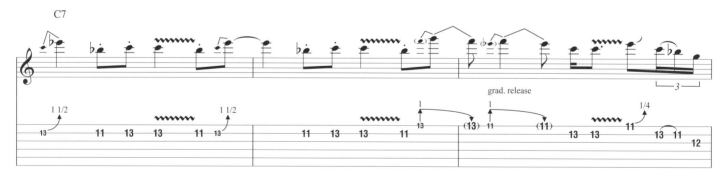

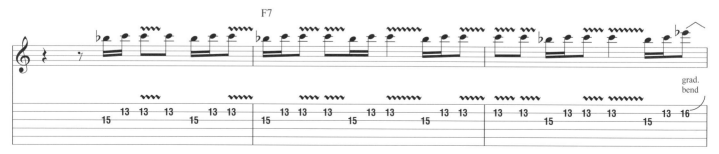

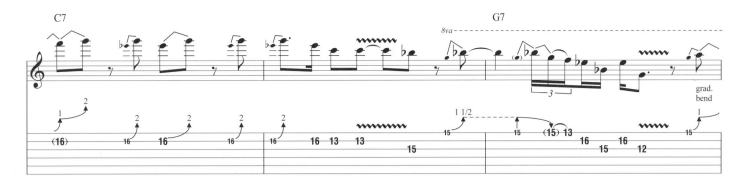

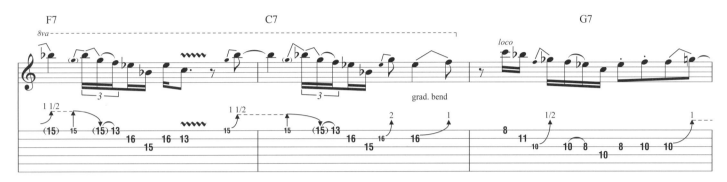

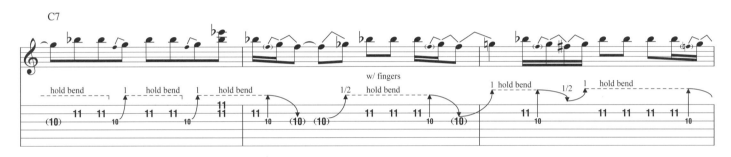

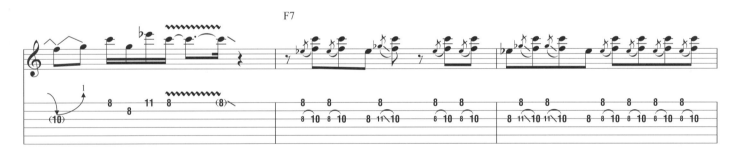

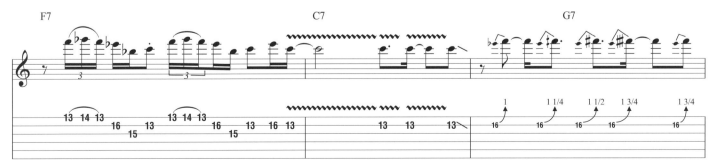

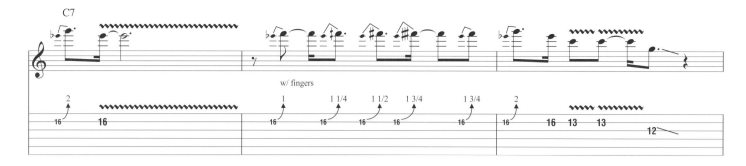

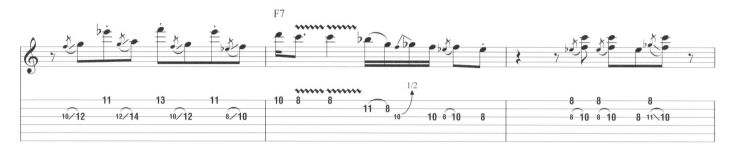

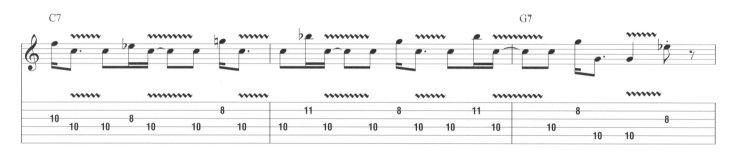

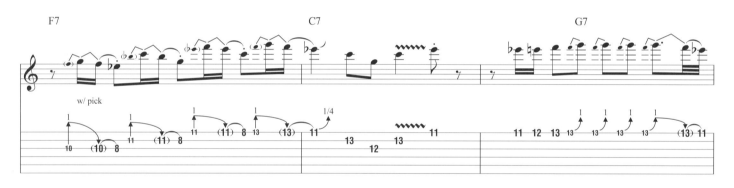

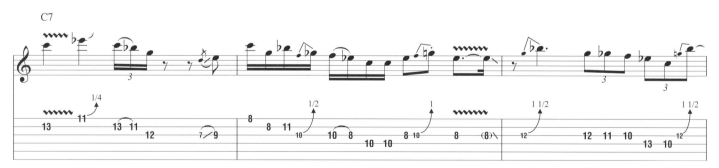

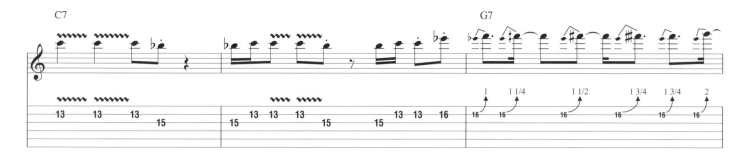

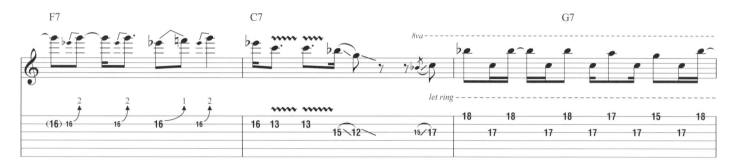

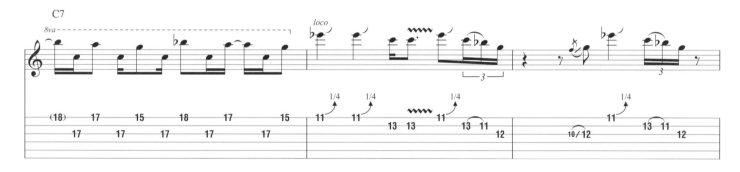

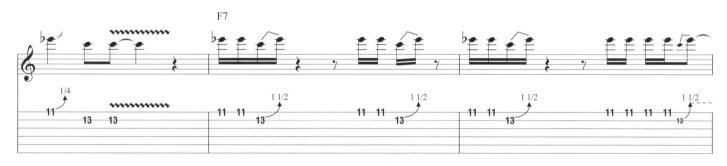

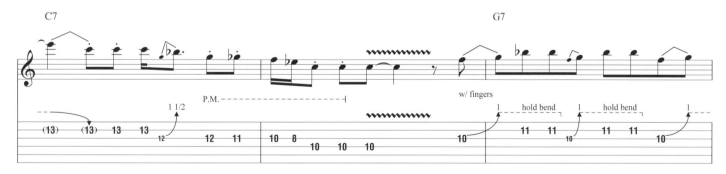

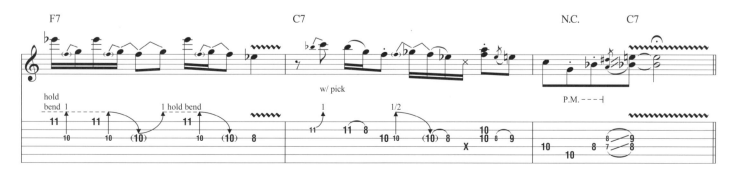

Chapter 6: Fingerpicking and Damping

Example 41
(2:07)

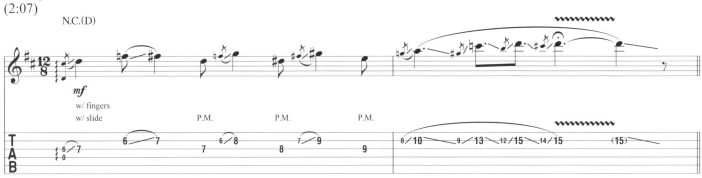

Example 42
(2:18)

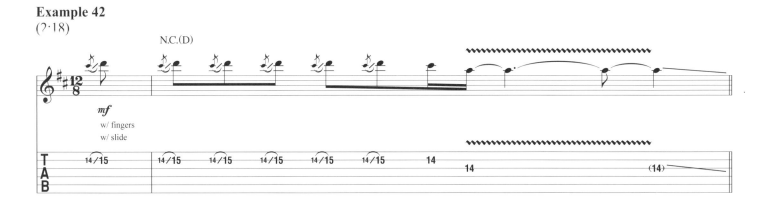

Example 43: Elmore James
(2:37)

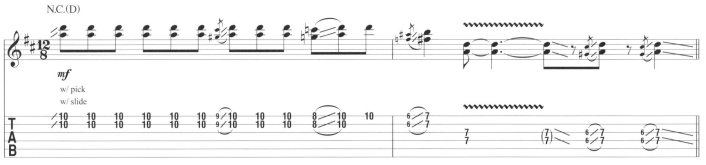

Example 44: Muddy Waters
(2:48)

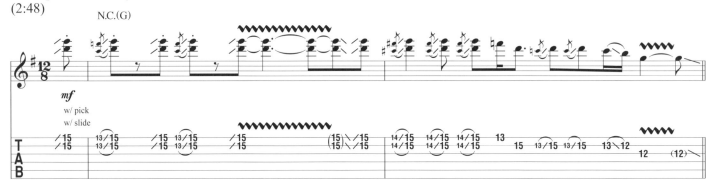

Example 45

(3:52)

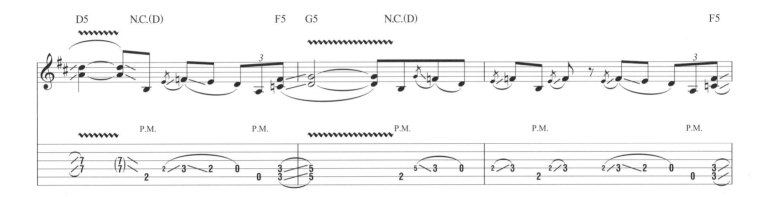

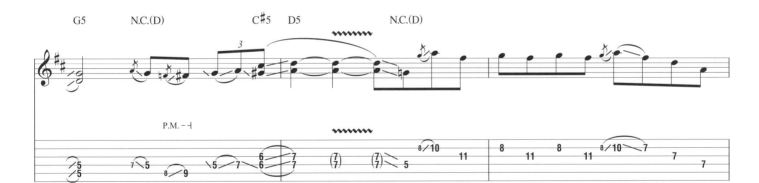

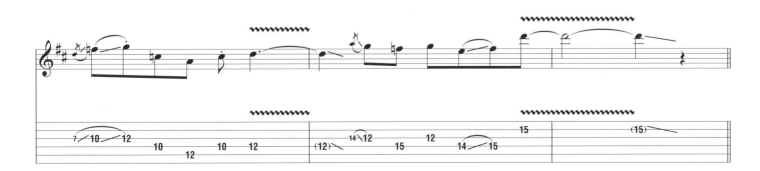

Example 46
(5:12)

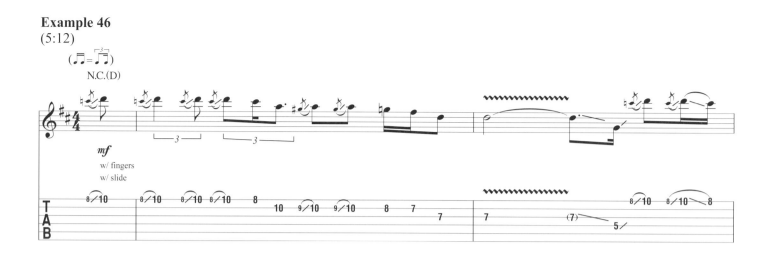

Example 47
(6:11)

Example 48
(6:30)

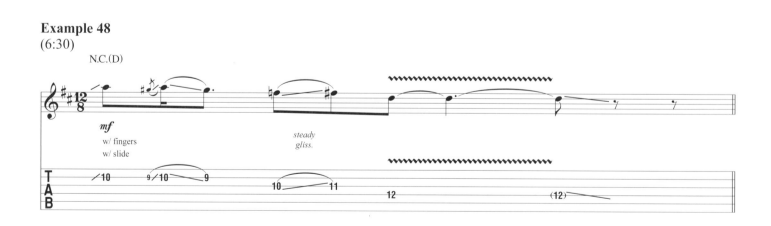

Chapter 7: Light Touch

Example 49

(1:11)

Example 50

(2:17)

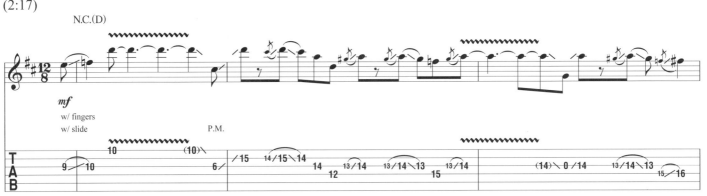

Example 51

(3:08)

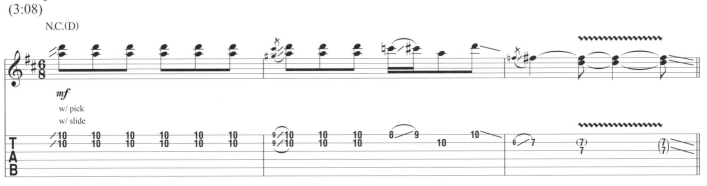

Example 52

(3:22)

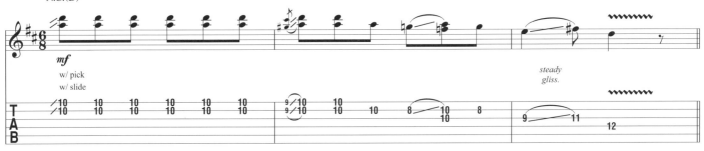

Chapter 8: Choosing Strings for Tone

Example 53A: G String
(:10)

Example 53B: D String
(:13)

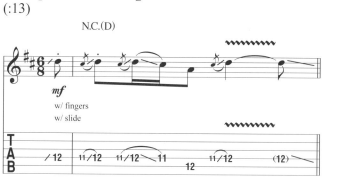

Example 54A
(:42)

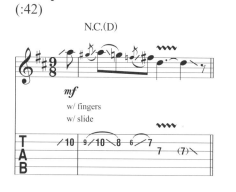

Example 54B
(:48)

Example 54C
(:54)

Example 55
(1:35)

Example 56
(2:17)

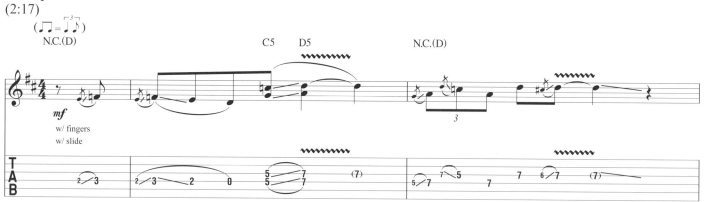

Chapter 9: Emulating Open-Tuned Sounds in Standard Tuning

Example 57

(:16)

Example 58

(:30)

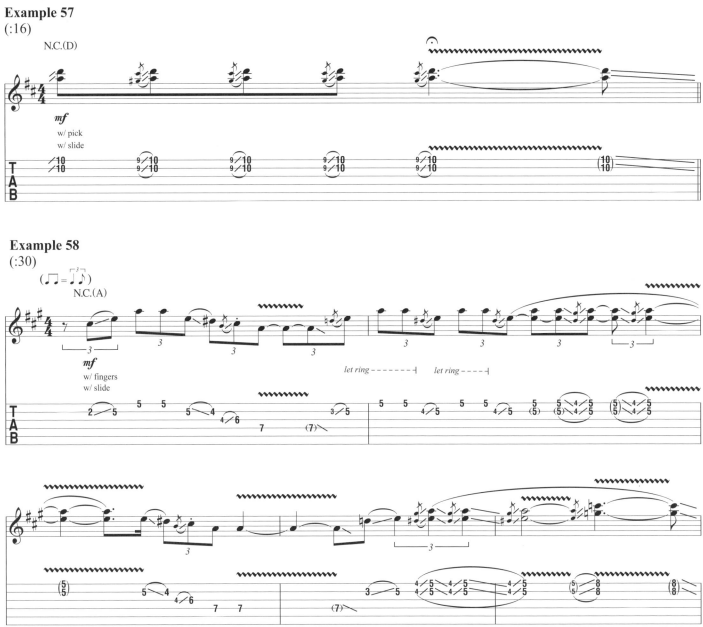

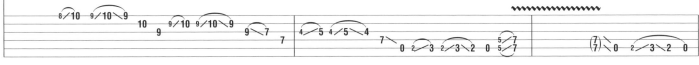

Example 59
(1:46)

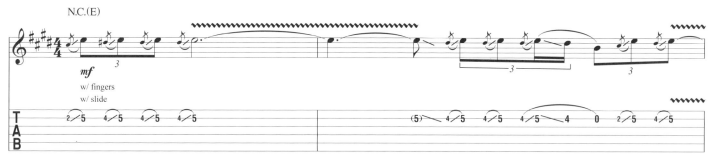

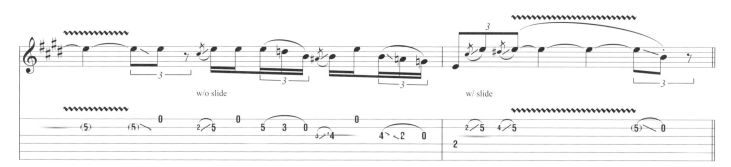

Example 60
(2:04)

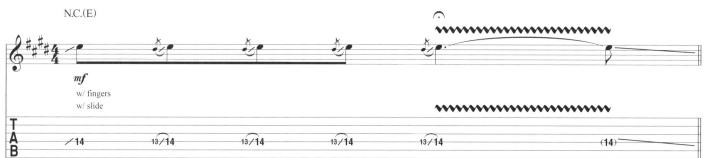

Example 61
(2:59)

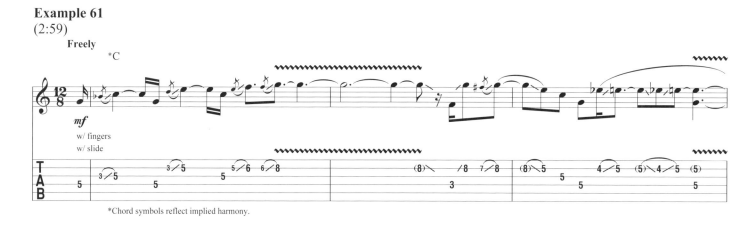

*Chord symbols reflect implied harmony.

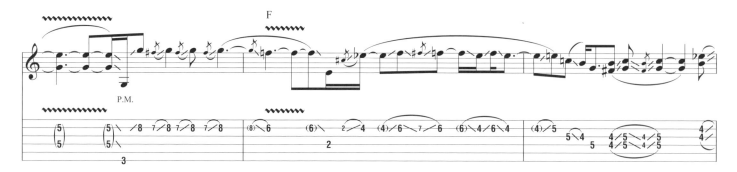

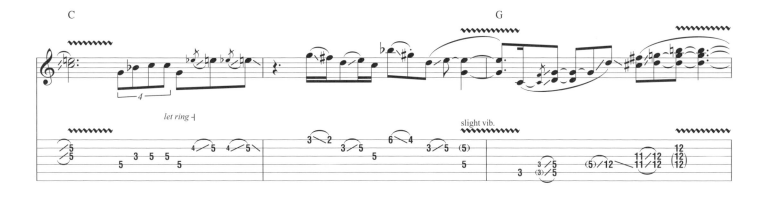

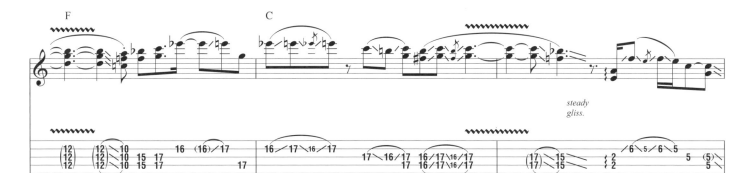

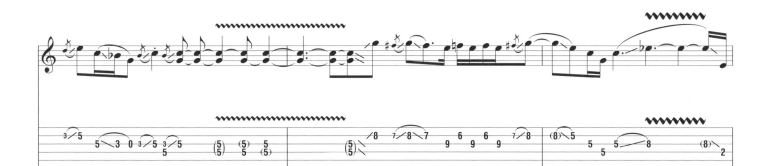

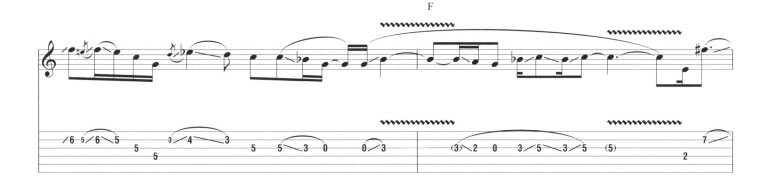

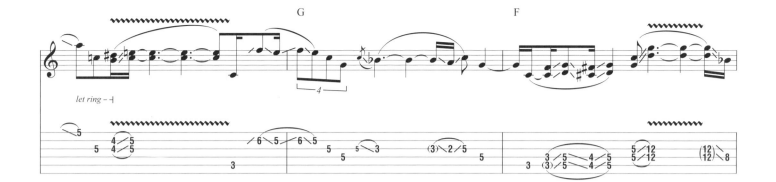

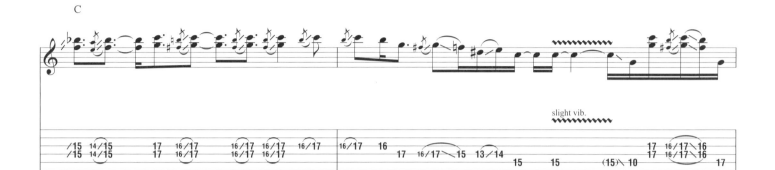

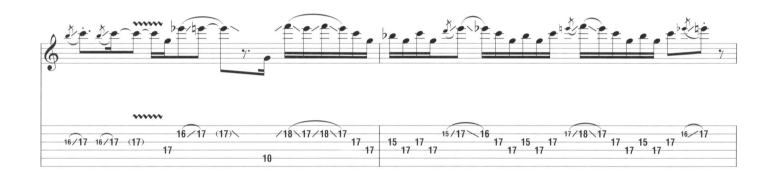

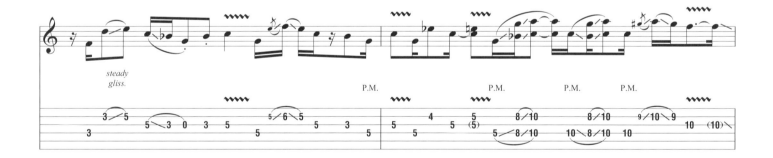

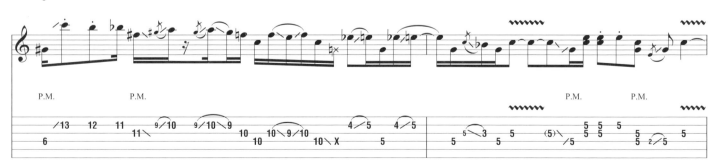

C

G   F

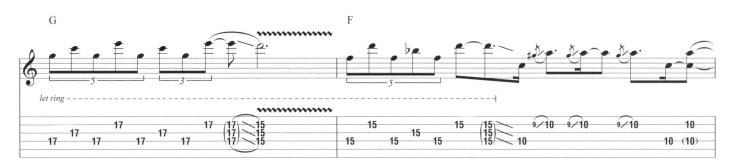

C

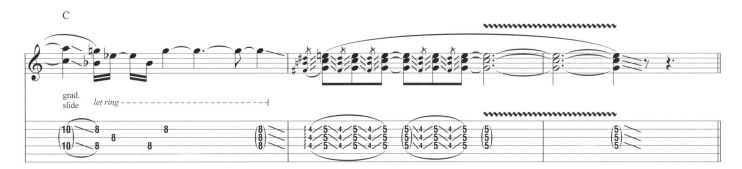

Chapter 10: Vibrato and Intonation

Example 62

(1:00)

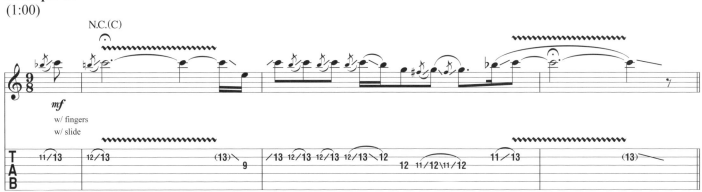

Example 63: Delta Blues Vibrato

(1:20)

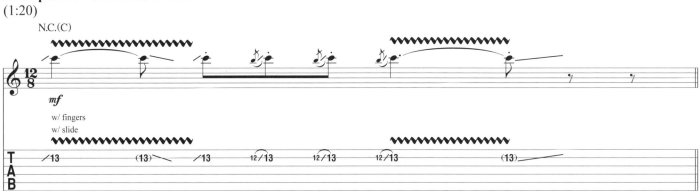

Example 64
(1:36)

*Played as even-eighth notes.

Example 65
(2:05)

Example 66
(2:13)

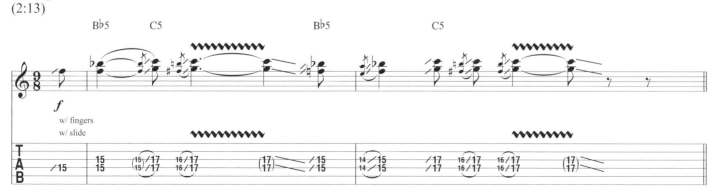

Example 67

(2:47)

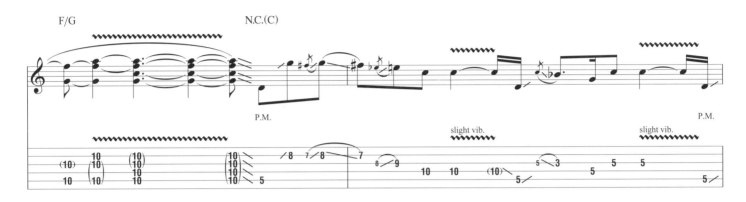

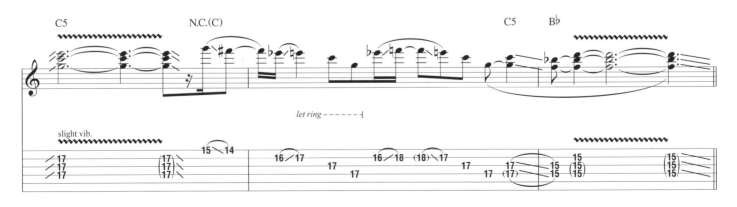

Example 68
(3:34)

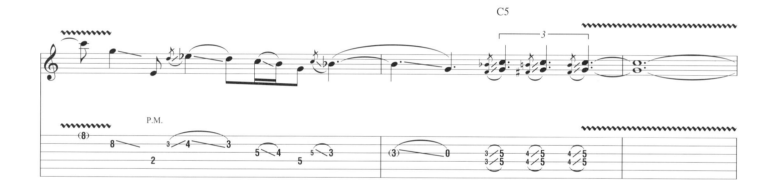

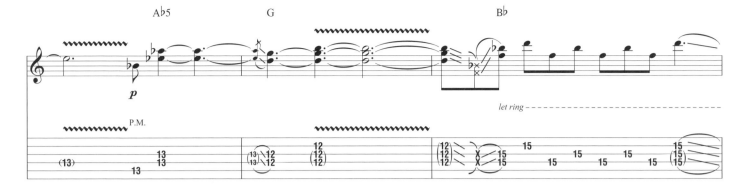

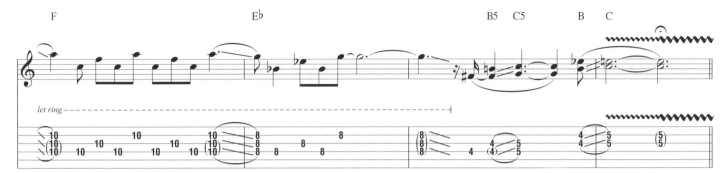

Example 69

(5:25)

Example 70

(7:28)

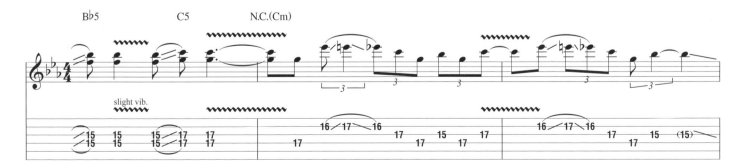

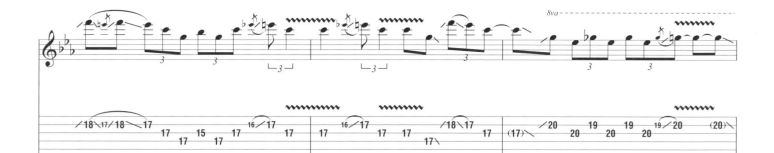

*Hypothetical fret location.   **Played as even 8th notes.

Example 71
(8:29)

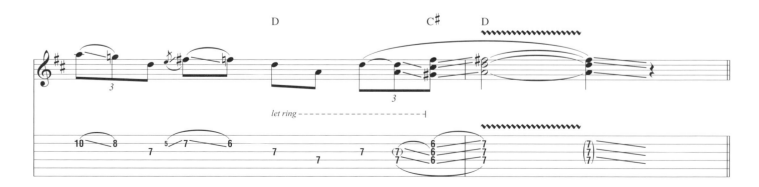

Example 72
(8:53)

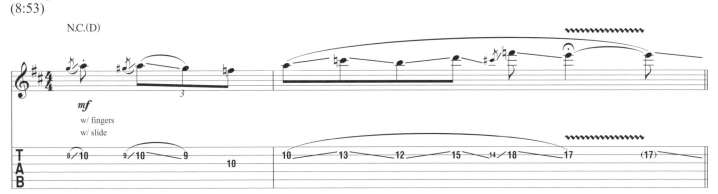

Example 73
(9:40)

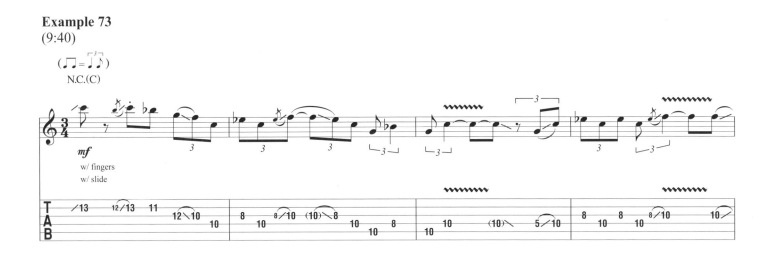

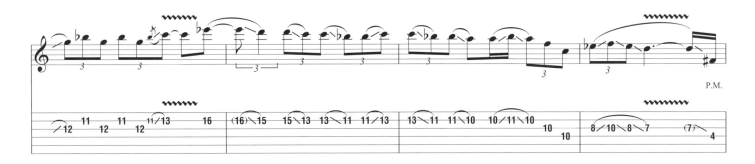

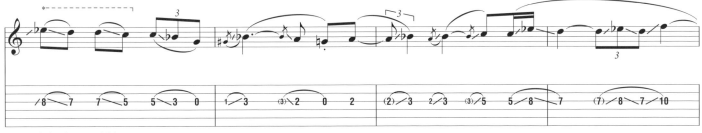

*Played as even-eighth notes.

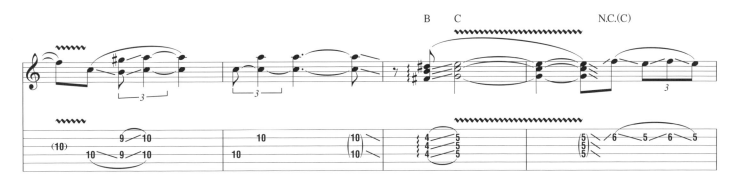

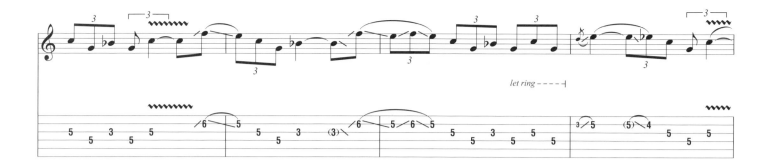

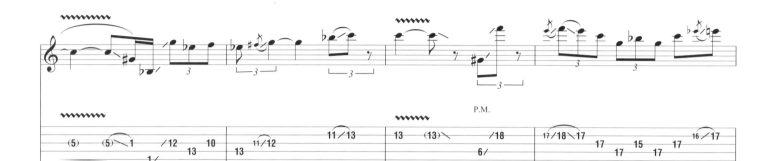

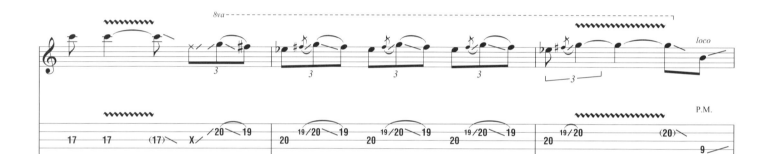

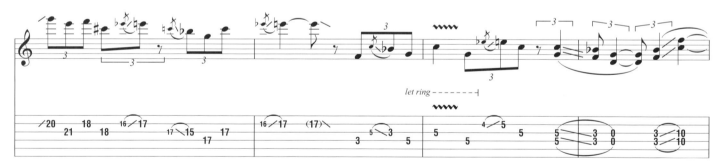

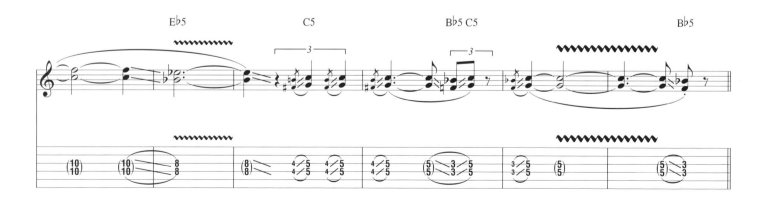